The Maine Coon Life Books

Credits

Starring: Artemis Morgana and Apollo Merlin ⊚@themainecoonlife

Photographs and book design: Reka Komoli ⊚@londowl

Text: Peter B Lloyd and Reka Komoli

Creative assistant: Nikolett Varga ⊚@csacsiga

Lent a big helping paw: Buster and Bertie ⊚@buster_and_bertie

Thanks to all the pawsies who supported us and believed in us!

First edition, June 2018

©2018 Reka Komoli - The Maine Coon Life Books

www.themainecoonlife.com

ISBN: 978-1-902987-32-3

Printed in the USA

The Maine Coon Life

'I was just wondering, Artemis, what were you expecting when I first arrived?'

'Hoomans said they had an *exciting* surprise for me. I was picturing a tiara, or a soft toy, or special tuna treats, … and then they produced a walking, pooping ball of ginger fluff.'

'I see. And after they gave you the fluff-ball, I arrived, yes?'

'You *were* the ball of fluff, Apollo!'

'Me, a fluff-ball? Hmm, then it seems I've changed a lot since that time, haven't I?'

'Only in size. A Maine Coon can't change its stripes.'

(Straining to look at his back.) 'But, but Artemis! I'm not a stripy cat!'

'It's a figure of speech, numbskull. Didn't they teach you rhetoric in the Feline University?'

'Oh, we had no time for any arty-party literature. It was all engineering and hard science.'

'Here we go again! I suppose you're now about to tell me the teleportation yarn once more?'

'But it's true! How else can you explain the way we arrived in the hoomans' house?'

'Well, I was carried here snuggled inside Hoomum's jacket, warm and cosy against the wind and rain. But I am sure you didn't come by that route as you would have pooped and parped the whole way.'

'Exactly. I teleported from outer space. I went to the Cat Extraterrestrial lab where they studied me, and then hoomans put me in the special isolation chamber for ET cats.'

'Your imagination is utterly baroque. That 'chamber' was a bathtub. You arrived with fleas and had to stay in the bathtub while the medicine took effect.'

'Whatever. But after I was released from the isolation chamber, I was introduced to you on the big red sofa and you should have seen your face drop! What a scaredy cat!'

'Scared my whiskers! Why would I be afraid of a walking fluff-ball? I was yucked out.'

'It took you thirty thousand and seven hundred days even to shake paws with me! Scaredy cat! Scaredy cat! Artemis was afraid of the ginger fluff-ball!'

'Despite your pong, I did my best to accept you into my clean, well-organised home. And you repaid me by chewing through the string of my cherished dragonfly toy!'

'Sorry, I thought the string was meant for chewing. But your life hasn't been boring since I came, has it?'

'True, we've had some wild times and memorable adventures, my funny little brother.'

Fluff-ball

Thug life

Baby Grumpuss

On my way home

Snuggle time

What is this thing, anyway?

'When you think about our travels, ginger munchkin, where do you think of?'

'So many places! We went to ...'

'I mean real places, not your interstellar fantasies.'

'Oh, those! Well, I had most fun in Las Vegas. Do you remember when Hoomum went to the Grand Canyon for her birthday, and we trashed the motel room?'

'O for the sake of tuna! You behaved like a catnip-crazed rock star! The room was covered in shredded loo paper like confetti! And how many bags of treats did you rip open?'

'What happens in Vegas stays in Vegas. It's just between you and me, right?'

'You thought hoomans didn't notice?'

'All right, between you, me, and them only. So what place do you think about, Artemis?'

'For me, the best expedition was when hoomans took me hunting in Central Park!'

'Posing more like! I saw you on that rock, showing your left profile and then your right. Asking Hoomum which pose was most lynx-like! Giving her your "fierce eyebrow" look!'

'I was just showing her what a brave cat looks like.'

'You weren't exactly brave when they bought the cooling fan, were you?'

'We were desperate to cool down in that New York heatwave! You even hopped into the shower! And I did jump when they turned on that big fan! But, after surviving the sweltering Big Apple, our most glamorous travel-time was in Paris, *n'était-ce pas*? Ooh la la!'

'And the *sweetest* travel-time was sitting on the bank of the Little Danube in Hungary, watching the birdies and fishies in the wild. Maine Coons in nature, hey!'

'It was so peaceful. Except when that noisy propeller-driven aeroplane dived towards us. Hoodad said "It's all right, kitties", but it kept coming! No wonder we both scarpered.'

'Ha ha! Did you see Hoodad running after us, tripping over the broken slats in the wooden bridge? And that was the day Hoomum caught those fishies and put them in a jar, trying to convince us they were food. Anyone could see they were living things!'

'Apart from the aeroplane incident, the garden was Edenic, wasn't it? Sweet and peaceful. Before the long exodus to Essex.'

'But that exodus was fun. On the road trip back to England, I was so curious to watch the scenery from the window, I forgot to eat my breakfast *and* dinner. So much to see!'

Can I stick my head out?

Les gardiens du Louvre

Bonne nuit, Paris!

'Artemis, why do we always observe the hooman holidays and they never observe ours?'

'What do you mean 'observe the holidays', Apollo? We take it easy *every* day.'

'Well, we always get dressed up for *Christmas, Halloween, Easter, St Patrick's Day, St George's Day, Thanksgiving, Fourth of July, May the Fourth*, and, and, and ...'

'But *Thanksgiving* and *Fourth of July* are U.S. holidays. You can't celebrate them here.'

'Oh yes I can, Miss Twitchy-Whiskers! I am a cosmopolitan cat and I can celebrate the holiday of any country I have lived in.'

'And *May the Fourth* is made up. It's just that Jedi thingy.'

'Artemis, all holidays are made up by somebody. Or you think they grow on trees?'

'Well, I like *Halloween* best. I can be really fierce and scare everyone!'

'You do that every day, Artemis! You even scare me when you are in a grumpy mood.'

'Maybe so, but when I don my Countess Dracula costume even the hoomans run in terror! I used to sit in the window of the house in Wivenhoe and give them the Evil Eye!'

'Are you sure they weren't just running for the train?'

'Nonsense. They started running when I hissed and showed them my fangs.'

'Anyway, I prefer my Paddington Bear costume.'

'We're talking about high days and holidays. There is no *National Paddington Bear Holiday*.'

'There ought to be! Everyone would give each other marmalade sandwiches on that day!'

'And what did you mean about cat holidays? Cats don't need holidays as we are at the apex of the social order.'

'Well, what about the *Grand Festival of Tuna*? And the *Day of Catnip*? And the *Twelve Days of Feather Toys*? Or the *Night of Long Tummy Rubs*?'

'What in the name of furriness are you talking about? Those are fake holidays!'

'Shush! Don't tell Hoomum! I've been saying to her that I can't do any photo shoots on certain days because they're National Cat Holidays.'

'Did she believe you?'

'I think so. She gave me extra treats. She must've thought that was the right thing to do on *Treatmas Day*. Hoomans are so gullible, they believe whatever we meow at them.'

'Hmm. Probably she was just bribing you to stop you lounging around like a liquid cat.'

I am the terror in the window!

The Countess and Count

Trick or treat?

¡Feliz Día de Muertos!

May the force be with you!

Is it Full Moon tonight?

'So you think you're a meowrvellous huntress, eh, Artemis? Well I've hunted 728 insects today. While you were hunting bubbles in the paddling pool. Hee hee!'

'Oh, fluff off, ginger brain. I was training myself in meowrtial arts.'

'You're seriously comparing chasing bubbles to the noble discipline of Cat-Fu?'

'You're just displaying your ignorance. It takes lightning-fast reactions to catch bubbles.'

'But you can't eat them if you do catch any bubbles! At least I can eat the bugs I catch.'

'Yuck! You mean you actually eat those disgusting bluebottles and house flies?'

'They're super succulent. But you'll have to catch your own if you want a taste.'

'Euw! I saw that Hoodad tried to stop you eating one of them!'

'That's right, there was a bright yellow-and-black stripy one, I really wanted to taste it. It was buzzing a lot, too. But Hoodad pushed me away. I think he wanted to eat it himself.'

'Since when do hoomans eat bumble bees?! O you cat of little brain! Don't you remember what happened on our first day in Aporka? We were both banned from the balcony because *you* wanted to play floofball with a bumble bee?'

'Holy catnip! Was that bug the same thing? Ouch! Good job I didn't eat it then!'

'You complain about hoomans being dippy but you really are slow sometimes.'

'You know what I like most about sunny days? After a day's hunting in the sun, there's nothing better than lounging in the deck chair, waiting for Hoomum to bring the tunatini. Or hiding under the big shady leaves of the bushes, and watching hoomans getting agitated because they thought one of us had run away from the garden again.'

'I never "ran away". I was in hot pursuit of the feral felines who were trying to invade our garden. It was a military operation, constantly patrolling the perimeter at the garden fence.'

'And you appointed me Private Poops! It was great teamwork keeping the garden clear of inbound cats. But ... couldn't we have just played with the ferals sometimes?'

'Play with the riff-raff? Meowngle with *hoi polloi*?'

'Oh come on, you snob cat! The ferals are the same as us but homeless. And you're not as posh as you think! I've seen you poop in the garden instead of the cat litter! Like a wildling!'

'Apollo! How dare you watch me when I am going about my private business!'

'Well, why can't you just enjoy the garden as a recreational facility not as a bathroom?!'

Follow nature, focus inside!

So near, yet so far!

Private Poops, prepare to attack!

Watcha looking at?

Gotcha!

So long and thanks for all the fish!

'I detect that you are sitting on a crime scene, Pawtson.'

'Great Scott! How on Earth do you know that, Holmes?'

'Elementary! I'm sporting a deerstalker hat and matching raincoat, so I must be cosplaying Sherlock Holmes, which means that you're playing Dr Pawtson. But I observe from the bits of kibble on your mouth that you are a clumsy cat and would park your pawsterior on vital clues. As I do not see any clues around you, I deduce that you must be sitting on them.'

'I say, Holmes, you're right! I'm sitting on a chewed-up phone cable! It's a clue!'

'For the love of tuna, Apollo, can't you behave? You've already been caught by the pawlice once for cable chewing. And you've been at it again.'

'How in the world do you know it was me who dunnit?'

'Again, elementary! You are the only potential culprit here. Obviously *I* don't chew cables.'

'Not guilty! I've been framed! Batman and Superman will clear my name.'

'We *are* Batman and Superman! Remember when we sat on the roof and scanned the horizon for villains and super-villains, you were Batman and I was Superman.'

'We were so good at it, we scared away all the villains. We didn't spot a single outlaw.'

'But I don't see how Batman and Superman are going to get you off the hook this time.'

'Hmmm. Maybe not ... but I have an alibi.'

'A likely story! Well, go on then, dazzle me with your meowrvellous alibi.'

'I'm ... I'm Iron Man! And Iron Man can eat cables as if they were noodles! Gotcha!'

'That's not an alibi, numbskull. You just admitted to chewing the cable. Secondly, Iron Man is not made of iron. He is just a hooman wearing a metal suit. He. Doesn't. Eat. Metal.'

'Er, well, be that as it may, ... I didn't do it and you can't prove it anyway.'

'As Captain Ameowrica, I am sworn to defend cables against feline felons! I will prevail over you in this Sibling War that you are waging!'

'Eeek! Then I'll make the cable vanish with my wand and a spell I learnt at Meowgwarts!'

'Will you stop mixing up the cosplays! We've been so many characters—Little Red Riding Hood and the Wolf, House MD, Fantastic Beasts—it's hard to keep track of who we are.'

'That's right ... maybe I could cosplay you, and you me?'

'No way! I would never play you, not for all the tuna in the ocean!'

Have I gone mad?

42!

Double, double toil and trouble!

How long is forever?

Wing-gar-dium Levi-o-sa!

NiP MarmaLaDe

I love marmalade!

'Rainy days are a mixed blessing, don't you think, Miss Prickly Whiskers?'
'Rainy days are just wet, Apollo. And the name's Artemis to you.'
'Well, we can't play in the garden, but we do find lots of pastimes to do indoors!'
'What, like watching Netflix you mean? Well, it's a good second-best to garden playtime.'
'Netflix is well cool. But there's other things on the pawputer. Like playing *Assassin's Creed.*
Or searching for new hoomans when they've been naughty and we vow to get rid of them.'
'Hee hee! Yes, judging hoomans and giving them hard stares is a great hobby.'
'And punishing them by taking their plastic thing and ordering pizza with anchovies.'
'That was *you* who stole their credit card! *I* draw the line at criminal activity.'
'Do you now? Well what about when we were catnip smugglers hiding in a secret den with
our black hoodies? You were revelling in the thug life!'
'Come off it, Apollo, we were just play-acting at peddling catnip. It was a cardboard box,
dummy! We both like boxes, but only *you* pretend a box is a nip den!'
'I'm glad our hoomans realise how important boxes are to our zen, and keep us well supplied.'
'Why do you suppose hoomans never seem to like sitting in boxes?'
'Go figure. Nobody really knows what's going on in the mind of a hooman.'
'That's so true, Apollo. For example, sometimes I think the rain has stopped and I ask
hooman to open the garden door so I can do a quick—'
'A quick poop!'
'—patrol, but as soon as my front half is out of the door I realise it's too wet to go out, so of
course I stop half way. That rude Hoodad starts whinging about it and even pushes me out!'
'You're always dithering. Like when you started your *World Domination* project, and before
we'd conquered a single city you decided you wanted to snuggle up in Hoomum's lap.'
'It was a strategic pawse. I have a clear vision of taking control of everything. You know
that I control this household. Just extrapolate! I'll control the hood, the city, … the planet!'
'Yes, of course you will, Artemis. Anyway, it's still raining, so even our plan to go glamping
in the garden is ruined. But … hey, let's pitch the tents and glamp in the living room.'
'Yes! And Hoodad has lit the fire, so we can really feel like we're camping outdoors.'
'Marshmallows cooked in the fire! All the fun of camping … which no rain can dampen!'

There is no wi fi signal!

When will it stop raining?

Could you pipe down?

'You coward! You always run and hide when Hoomum announces a bath-time for us!'

'If you weren't squealing like a piggy so much, you'd notice that I am very stoical. I just sit there quietly and let Hoomum get on with the ablutions. Not like you.'

'Well, I just don't like baths. I had aquatic traumas when I was a kitten.'

'That's an understatement. You scratch and wriggle to get out of being washed. You even bit Hoomum once. How did I end up with such a rebellious and undisciplined brother?'

'I had bad experiences when I first arrived in the hoomans' flat. But I am getting braver with water. Whenever Hoomum has a bath, I get my fishies out to hunt in the tub!'

'You really are an embarrassment to catkind with your hunting of little plastic fish.'

'But they have tiny electric motors and they zip around, and some of them have flashing lights, and … and the jellyfish has a remote control so Hoomum makes it go …'

'Apollo!'

'Yes, Artemis?'

'You're a Maine Coon. You're supposed to hunt real things not plastic toys.'

'So what? It's the best fun. I like it so much! I even dip my paws into the bath water to catch the fishies while they're swimming around. Sometimes I come so close to falling in!'

'Oh well, that would be a disaster wouldn't it? Full immersion in five inches of water. Anyway, If you were a bit cleaner you wouldn't need so much washing. Count how many times Hoomum has had to clean my pawsterior in three years: zero! Now count how many times Hoodad has had to clean your dirty bumhole? Just about every week or two!'

'It's not my fault! I have a very fluffy backside. And the litter box is so small. I can't always manage keep my rear end clean and tidy.'

'I'm bigger than you, and I manage it! Almost the only time Hoomum has had to wash me was when I stepped in some poop that you left lying around in the litter box.'

'Hmm. Anyway, you look really silly when you're all wet after a bath.'

'I beg your pawdon? Neither of us looks our best when we're wet and bedraggled.'

'That's true, but you look sillier than I do. You look like a bowling pin! Hee hee!'

'Huh. At least it feels cosy when Hoomum wraps us up in a soft towel to keep warm.'

'Mmm, yeah! All cwtched up, as Hoodad says.'

Apollo shall suffer my revenge!

Feline Torpedo

You will not escape my fury!

I regret nothing!

Drowned rat

Would I win the wet shirt gig?

'Sometimes I wonder whether the rest of the world thinks in a funny sort of way, Artemis.'

'Only *you* would have such an abstruse thought, Apollo. What are you alluding to?'

'Everyone kept saying how meowrvellously wonderful snow is. All those cartoon pictures depicting it as soft and bouncy like a marshmallow. All those cheerish Christmas cards with hooman cubs playing in the snow.'

'Ah yes, I know what you mean. The wintry reality was quite different from that image, as we now know. The first thing you notice about snow is: it's cold.'

'... and it's wet. And cold again.'

'And our paws just sink right into it. All the way up to our tummies.'

'It's the worst thing ever. Snowy days are much worse than rainy days.'

'What made it worse was hoomans' attitude. Getting us all excited with "Look kitties, it's your first ever snow!" And shoving us into the back garden to play. Play! Ha! Play in that horrible cold, wet, yucky stuff that sticks to the fur. Yeah, right.'

'My toe beans got so cold, I had to keep licking them to keep them warm.'

'And my tummy fur got so caked in snow I looked like the Abominable Snowcat.'

'Those hoomans were laughing and saying, "You're Maine Coons! You're meant to enjoy the snow". I can't believe how ignorant hoomans are. The word "cat" comes from ancient Babylonian, and means "warm and cosy". It does not mean "Freezing your toe beans off".'

'I don't even know why they have snow. I mean, what's it for?'

'I think it just comes. Like birdies and feral cats. It just comes out of the blue and melts away. There's no reason for it. But when it does come, it's time to stay indoors.'

'I never want to walk in it again. No matter how excited those brainless hoomans get.'

'At least we looked good in the photos! Our fur bristles up and we look so big and tough.'

'That's true. And, to give her credit, Hoomum did suffer like us, lying on her tummy in the snow to take our pictures.'

'But Hoodad was such a wimp—putting on his big boots and his overcoat before stepping into the garden.'

'We're much more resilient than he is.'

'What do you expect? He's not a cat, is he?'

Snow is fun, they said ...

Won't move, can't move!

I'll save you, peanut butter tosie!

Is this what snow is?

Shall we go back to bed now?

Frozen toe beans, anyone?

'In my kitchen, I am La Chef and you Le Commis Chef. In tuna tasting, my palate is the more perceptive. In book reviews, the incisive ideas always come from *moi*, not *toi*. In drawing, my works are inspired, yours merely mechanical. Even in colouring books, I outshine you. No offence, Apollo, but really ...'

'You do know it's all in the eye of the beholder, don't you, Miss Twitchy Tail?'

'Oh, so is that the limit of your artistic critique?'

'Taste, beauty, aesthetics. It's all subjective. And my subjectivity is as valid as yours.'

'No it isn't. What do you think art is, ginger-head? Personal whim? No, it is a nexus of transmission and development embedded in a socio-political and art-historical context.'

'Fluff off, fancy-pants. We both have degrees from the University of Feline Arts and Sciences. You're no better than I am, we just followed different disciplines.'

'Genuine art relies on the eye and the paw, not on machinery, which seems to be your *forte*. My paintings are *bona fide* art, your pawtographs are mere mechanical reproductions.'

'As a left-brain sort of cat, I acknowledge that I have a talent for technical things ...'

'What are you talking about, a 'left-brain cat'? You don't have any brain at all!'

'I was trained in science, which uses the left hemisphere of the brain. But to keep my brain well balanced, I study right-brain things. Creative, arty-party things. Like taking pictures.'

'But you're not exactly creative are you? More of a point-and-click snapper.'

'Creativity is a matter of personal expression. As you know, I took up the camera because Hoomum was getting too busy to take pictures of us, and I have trained myself to emulate her skill while developing my own visual style.'

'But, but ... when you click the shutter you have no paw in the act of creation!'

'You have such a blinkered view of pawtography, Artemis. The composition, the lighting, the precise timing, the angle of view, the filter, the camera settings, they combine to form a means of creative expression comparable to your brush dipped in paint.'

'Let me give you an example that illustrates my point. When we go camping at Clawstonbury, it is the presence of the artistes that makes it worth while and authentic. Just playing back a recording would be inauthentic. Likewise, a pawtograph can't be authentic art!'

'You have so much to learn about the expressive power of the lens. Wake up, Artemis!'

Doctor and Doctor

You moved your whiskers again!!!

Artemis, say tunatini!

Tuna-tasting class

Did they publish our letter?

We asked for a laptop not pencils!

'Apollo, I have a confession to make.'

'Oh, goody!'

'Everybody thinks that I'm a terribly fierce, rough, tough miniature Lynx, yes?'

'Er, well that's the persona you like to project, yes.'

'So, the thing is, I really like snuggling in bed. Beddy time is quite special to me.'

'Awww. I thought so. I enjoy beddy stories too. Especially when Hoodad reads us stories when we're curled up in bed. His story of the Bogey Dog is a real killer-diller thriller!'

'I prefer heart-warming stories like *Winnie-the-Pooh*, although you seem to like spine-chilling Gothic ones, such as your *Frankenstein* and *Willard*.'

'It's a pity Hoodad doesn't read to us as often as he should. But at least we can read quietly by ourselves now. You were very engrossed in that book last night. What was it?'

'*De Luxe Grooming for Celebrity Cats*'

'You're going to groom your tongue off one of these days. I was reading *Exploring Extraterrestrial Civilisations*. The author has a theory that life on Mars is almost certainly more feline than hooman. If there is life on Mars, that is, which we don't know yet ...'

'How can you sleep with your little head buzzing so much with wild ideas?'

'Well, I do often wake up in the middle of the night and think of pawsome projects. I find that I sleep better after one of our relaxing Netflix evenings.'

'I agree. An exciting adventure story with a happy ending. Just right for getting off to sleep.'

'It's very sweet snuggling up with my big sister in bed and drifting off to sleep.'

'Awww. But will you promise to clean your bum properly before coming to bed from now on? Cleanliness is next to catliness, you know!'

'Why are you always having a dig at me, even when I am being sweet and reminiscing about how harmonious our life is?'

'Well why don't you groom yourself like your mother taught you?'

'I didn't get as far as the grooming lessons. I was teleported away from my mummy before she could teach me all the tricks of grooming.'

'I'm sorry about that. But couldn't you learn from me how to look after yourself?'

'I do, Artemis, I do! All the grooming I know, I learned by emulating you, big sis!'

But we aren't sleepy yet!

Give us a break!

Sweet dreams!

Who needs pillows?

Sharing dreams

Ready for a beddy-story!

'Fluff off, Artemis, I'm a cat not a hooman!'

'All I said was, "We should contribute more to the upkeep of the household by working".'

'I don't mind doing gigs for museums and film premieres, or reviewing comics and books. But if I have to work for my tuna every day, how would I have time for my own projects?'

'You could do less catnapping?'

'No way! Without napping, when would I dream? And without dreams, what is life?'

'I thought you enjoyed working as official Post Office Cat at the London Postal Museum?'

'Absolutely! I loved riding the mail train, and inspecting the sorting machines, and snuggling with all the lovely staff in the office. But I prefer to do this as an occasional consultancy, not as regular employment. Jobs are for hoomans, not cats.'

'So you're now a Consulting Cat?'

'Purrcisely! In that gig we did for BBDO in Paris, we were a purrfessional team—inspired by my consulting experience to build a circular scratch pad out of cardboard; with your glamour; and hoomans doing the mechanical work. We delivered outrageously cute videos.'

'Don't ... *Do. Not.* ... underestimate the important role of my glamour. It was *my* ravishing looks that got us the photo-meowdelling work at the premiere of the Unikitty film.'

'You were such a poseur! But you see, your aloofness is a disadvantage in these situations. All the hooman starlets wanted to hold me, not you, because I'm—'

'—a cuddle addict!'

'I beg your pawdon! I just *like* cuddles and attention. And you don't. That's all.'

'Not true! I'm fine with hooman cuddles, I just don't like body contact with strangers!'

'At least there's no cause for social anxiety about strangers in the home-studio photo-shoots.'

'I agree. And we've done some fascinating work with Hoomum's promotional shoots—I liked that water fountain gig so much!'

'Did you ever realise it's for drinking not paddling? Anyway I rated the pet cam best.'

'Yeah, until you sabotaged it by sticking your paw into the treat ejector.'

'I'm sure I read in the instructions: click button for treats! I was trying hard to paw-click it.'

'I suppose eating treats is your way of coping with fame. Like when we were on the billboards in Wivenhoe train station and the whole town was talking about us for months!'

'I'm sure it was roe deer we saw in the field near Wivenhoe.'

'I don't think you'd recognise a roe deer if it face-bumped you.'

'But I have my field guide to British wildlife, I can recognise anything that moves.'

'You didn't recognise that cow when you tried to climb on its nose.'

'Well it wasn't moving. I was just chasing the flies. I didn't know there was a cow there.'

'It was right in front of us. Why didn't you look it up in your little book?'

'My book was packed up in my knapsack. And the flies were dancing before my eyes ...'

'Thankfully Hoodad ran and grabbed you before you jumped on the cow.'

'By the way, I *knew* Hoodad was teasing us when he said crossing that footbridge would take us into Zimbabwe.'

'No you didn't. Neither of us knew that Essex isn't next door to Africa'.

'*And* I knew he was teasing when he said we were sitting on the bank of the River Nile.'

'Oh fluff! You had no idea it was really the humble River Colne.'

'I knew it couldn't be the Nile because there were no hippopotamuses on the mud banks.'

'It's Hoodad's Welsh sense of humour. He thinks it's funny to tease cats about their limited knowledge of international geography.'

'I asked him: is Hampstead Heath closer to the North Pole than Essex is, as it's colder?'

'I think that's because it's in the clouds. We had to wear our scarves to keep warm.'

'Or is Central Park closer to the Equator? I couldn't believe how hot it was there.'

'I wasn't sure where Central Park was. After changing twice on the subway I lost my sense of direction. It seemed at least a thousand miles from Brooklyn.'

'I was wondering whether Central Park might be somebody's back garden, because it's in the middle of a city. Not like Wivenhoe where the city is inside the countryside.'

'Then what about Hampstead Heath? That's inside a city but we saw lakes and forests inside it, so it can't be someone's back garden. Can it?'

'I guess not. The world of hoomans sometimes seems to be a "riddle, wrapped in a mystery inside an enigma". It's interesting but extraordinarily complicated.'

'Not like our world, which makes perfect sense.'

'That's right, the Maine Coon life is the best of all!'

Border guard

I spy with my little eye ...

One little step for a feline ...

You said we'll be back by dinner!

Any birdies on the horizon?

What are those things?